CANDOO!

A PLAY

JAMES M. GUIHER

iUniverse, Inc.
New York Bloomington

Candoo!
A Play

No professional or nonprofessional performances of any kind or in any media of this play may be given without the permission of the author, who can be contacted at: jamesmguiher.com

iUniverse books may be ordered through booksellers or by contacting:

iUniverse
1663 Liberty Drive
Bloomington, IN 47403
www.iuniverse.com
1-800-Authors (1-800-288-4677)

ISBN: 978-1-4502-3227-2 (sc)
ISBN: 978-1-4502-3228-9 (ebook)

Printed in the United States of America

iUniverse rev. date: 06/07/2010

ACT I

The Acropolis.

ACT II

The same.

TIME: The present.

SETTING: The east facade of the Parthenon. Across about 2/3 of stage right are steps leading up to several of the northern-most Doric columns. Downstage are broken fragments from the temple. Stage left two small tents and a portable toilet. Several canvas director's chairs scattered about.

CHARACTERS

A.J. "CANDOO" JONES, a Texas oil man

MARBURY V. MADISON, his lawyer

ARTHUR J. JONES, JR., his son

GLORIA JONES, his sister

ELENA, a young Greek maiden

SHEIKH ABDUL OF SAUDI ARABIA

THE PRESIDENTE OF PARAGONIA

THE PRIME MINISTER OF JAPAN

A SAMURAI

ZEUS, king of the Greek gods

DR. ROWAN D. BEND, a psychiatrist

OLAF, a man in a white suit

With doubling, 8 actors can perform the play.

ACT I

From stage right in strides A.J. "CANDOO" JONES, a rich Texas oil man, dressed as a cowboy with boots, a Stetson hat, and a holstered pistol strapped to his right leg. He looks to be about 50 years old and has the gait of a man who has spent a lot of time on the back of a horse.

With him is his lawyer, MARBURY V. MADISON, pale and thin in a business suit, who is obviously uncomfortable being out of doors and in this strange place.

CANDOO

Well Marbury, here it is, the most famous building in the world, even more famous than the Alamo, and it all belongs to me.

MARBURY

I don't know why you bought this hill, nothing but busted ruins it'll cost a fortune to fix up.

CANDOO

What were we back in Houston, just another oil company. Here everyone will know we're somethin' special and they better start doin' business with us because we're on the way to growin' faster then Geronimo can run from Riley Creek back to the corral.

MARBURY

If you'd asked Geronimo about buying this place, even a dumb horse could have told you it was a stupid idea.

CANDOO

Be careful what you say about horses. When it comes to who's done more for the human race, horses or lawyers, horses win goin' away.

MARBURY

You know this deal has put us so far in debt we'll be lucky if we can ever pay it off.

CANDOO

You stick to seein' that we don't pay any taxes and let me worry about where we're goin' to get the money We will have to do some fixin' up before I can get Mabel over here.

MARBURY

No way your wife is ever going to live in one of these miserable tents.

CANDOO

They're not much worse than the shack she grew up in up in Oklahoma. We can put a swimming pool over there, a big one shaped like Oklahoma. She's always wanted a pool shaped like her dear old Oklahoma. Out here we can make a patio with some big umbrellas to keep the sun off, with a long marble bar at the side. Next to it an outdoor hot tub, one of those jacuzzi things that gets you all revved up for a good roll in the hay. Around back there'll be a nice corral for Geronimo.

MARBURY

Geronimo?

CANDOO

There's no road up here. You know my legs aren't much good for walkin'. I'll need a putting green so I can do some practicin'. It's my short game that needs workin' on. The inside? We'll leave that to Mabel. She'll want a big dining room to entertain all those snobs she loves to have in so she can show off her house.

MARBURY

She'll need air conditioning. It's hotter here than in Houston.

CANDOO

Yeah, but there's a nice breeze up here in the evening.

MARBURY

Without a road, how are we going to get down into town?

CANDOO

You can walk. The exercise will do you good.

MARBURY

What about Gloria? She can hardly walk across the room, even when she's sober.

CANDOO

I guess she'll have to stay up here. It'll keep her from spendin' all her money down in Athens.

MARBURY

You know this place was never designed to be lived in. It was a temple, a sacred building where the Athenians came up to worship their gods.

CANDOO

Back in the States, churches are being abandoned all over the country, turned into restaurants, bars, condos. It doesn't make sense to let them stand there and go to ruin.

MARBURY

But we don't need an expensive place like this. We could invest our money in something that will bring us a good return, like tankers or those oil fields in Russia or even some Las Vegas casinos.

CANDOO

I'm an oil man, Marbury. It's the business I know and the one I'm stickin' with. The Greek government was broke from puttin' on the last Olympics and was so desperate for cash they had to sell the Acropolis to keep from goin' bankrupt. And we got it at a bargain price.

MARBURY

How does anybody know what it's worth?

CANDOO

Some people think it's priceless, but take it from me, it's goin' to be a very good investment for us.

(ARTHUR enters. CANDOO'S son, he has an MBA from Stanford and, like most MBA's, thinks he's qualified to run a company right after he gets out of school. He too is wearing a business suit but with a cowboy hat.)

ARTHUR

Hey Pop, I just talked to Riyadh.

CANDOO

Who?

ARTHUR

The capital of Saudi Arabia. I've got the Saudis interested in a deal that can make us billions.

CANDOO

They've got plenty of oil. They don't need any more.

ARTHUR

This isn't oil.

CANDOO

Then I'm not interested.

ARTHUR

But this is a sure thing.

(GLORIA enters. The sister of CANDOO, attractive but seriously overweight, she is carrying a glass of bourbon and rather unsteady on her feet.)

GLORIA

Arty, brother dear, when are you going to fix up this place? Maybe you don't mind living like some poor Texas dirt farmer, but I do. I came over here to find myself a nice European gentleman, but he's sure as hell not going to come anywhere near this dump.

CANDOO

Patience, sister dear, we'll have all the VIP's of Europe lining up to visit us very soon.

GLORIA

(Taking a drink.)

Well I'm not spending another night in this hell hole. Get me a reservation at the best hotel in Athens.

MARBURY

Sorry, but we have no cash and we've maxxed out our credit.

ARTHUR

Pop, you've got to listen to me.

GLORIA

I can't stay here another night.

CANDOO

Silence! Shut up!

(He fires his pistol into the air. Two birds fall from the sky.)

MARBURY

It never fails. He always hits two birds with one shot.

CANDOO

Scram, beat it, all of you. I've got work to do.

> (They exit. CANDOO pulls out his cell phone, climbs the
> steps, punches some numbers.)

Hello Mabel, Yeah it's me. Look I want you to call Henry and have him go to the bank and get me some money. Yeah, he knows about my secret account there. We've run out of cash, and the Greeks won't accept any of our credit cards. They're givin' us a hard time because they're still pissed they had to sell the Acropolis to a foreigner. Yeah we've got enough food to last for a while. You want to know what? Drapes? What kind of drapes to order for the house? You know it's kind of unusual.. .it's the Parthenon. I don't think it has any windows. Well yeah, we can put some in. A pool? Sure, you bet. Big yeah, and you'll love it. A garden? I don't know. I don't think anything will grow up here. There's no dirt, nothin' but rocks and stones. Okay, I'll look into it.

> (ELENA appears. A lovely dark-haired young woman, she is
> wearing sandals and a white toga lined with a colorful frieze
> of Greek keys.)

CANDOO

Somebody's here. Gotta go. I don't know, a stranger. Talk to you later.

> (He turns to ELENA.)

Who are you? What are you doin' here? This is private property you know. No one is allowed up here without my permission.

ELENA

This hill is the sacred heart of Greece. From here, its spirit has spread to the entire civilized world. It belongs to all those who have been touched by the enlightened and illuminating soul of ancient Hellas.

CANDOO

Well right now it belongs to me, A.J. "Candoo" Jones.

ELENA

That cannot be.

CANDOO

I've got the papers to prove it, signed and sealed by the Greek government.

ELENA

The Greek government? They have no right to the Acropolis.

CANDOO

They sure do. My lawyer has checked it out.

ELENA

No mortal has such power, only the gods, and they will never let anyone take over the Acropolis, and certainly not a barbarian.

CANDOO

I'm not a barbarian. I'm an American from the great state of Texas, home of the Alamo, two American presidents, and the power-house Dallas Cowboys.

ELENA

All non-Greeks are barbarians.

CANDOO

Even the French? They'll sure be surprised to hear that.

ELENA

You must leave this hill.

CANDOO

I own it, and I'm stayin'.

ELENA

You cannot. You have no right...

CANDOO

Look lady, people have been tellin' me what to do all my life. If I had done what they said, I'd still be a poor rancher back in west Texas with too many debts and too few cattle. You gotta take risks, you gotta try to do what everybody else thinks is impossible, and if you believe you can you will, and you can't let anybody stop you.

ELENA

Such talk from a mere mortal will greatly anger the gods.

CANDOO

The gods? I don't give a damn what they think. I've been takin' chances and doin' things my way and that's why I'm here master of the Acropolis.

ELENA

I must warn you, the gods will punish such hubris.

CANDOO

Hu-what?

ELENA

Hubris. Extreme arrogance that threatens the very power of the gods.

CANDOO

Who are these gods you keep talkin' about?

ELENA

There is Zeus, the father of the gods, the most powerful one of all. There is Ares, the god of war...

CANDOO

Oh, those guys. I heard about them in school, just a bunch of old, fairy tales.

ELENA

Your ignorance is even more appalling than your vulgar barbarism.

CANDOO

I don't know who you.are, miss, but there's one thing you better understand. It's not what you know that counts, it's what you do and you can go tell that to Mr. Zeus and whoever else thinks he can stop me from gettin' what I want.

ELENA

I must warn you again, desist in this monstrous arrogance or you will be destroyed.

CANDOO

Your gods may think they're all powerful and they may have scared off a lot of people in the past but they've never met anyone like Candoo Jones, an American from the great state of Texas, so you go warn them that they better not mess with me of they'll be sorry.

(ELENA exits. ARTHUR enters.)

ARTHUR

Pop, Sheikh Abdul is here.

CANDOO

Who?

ARTHUR

Sheikh Abdul al-Ibaba of Saudi Arabia. He's an important member of their royal family. I told him about my proposal. He's very interested and wants to pursue it.

CANDOO

I told you I'm not interested.

ARTHUR

Saudi Arabia is a desert. They have lots of oil and no water. They can't develop and diversify their economy unless they get access to more water, a great deal more water.

CANDOO

Water? I'm an oil man.

ARTHUR

But here's the thing. Down in Antarctica, there's a huge ice sheet that keeps breaking off an endless supply of icebergs. We tow the icebergs up to Arabia and sell them to the Saudis.

CANDOO

Tow icebergs thousands of miles across the ocean? They'll melt down to nothing.

ARTHUR

An MIT professor has developed a covering that will protect them from the sun.

CANDOO

A ship runs into them and we'll be liable for millions of dollars in damages.

ARTHUR

Ships have radar and all kinds of electronic devices. They don't run into icebergs anymore. We get the Saudis dependent on our icebergs so if they jack up the price of oil, we cut off their water until they lower the price of oil. It'll guarantee we'll get the lowest price possible.

CANDOO

Where do we get the money for this kind of operation?

ARTHUR

We get the icebergs for nothing. And we make the Saudis pay for all the up-front costs. I figure we can make at least a 50% profit.

CANDOO

50%?

ARTHUR

Maybe more.

CANDOO

It's too risky.

ARTHUR

Pop, we've got to diversify. We've got to go beyond oil if we hope to make Candooco into a real world-class corporation.

CANDOO

An MBA five years out of Stanford and you think you know how to run the company.

ARTHUR

We've got to expand into a conglomerate involved in all kinds of industries. If you don't grow today, you don't last very long.

CANDOO

We've done fine so far. The Acropolis, the most famous address in the world, and it's all mine.

(MARBURY appears right with the SHEIKH. ARTHUR gestures for them to come in.)

ARTHUR

Pop, I want you to meet Sheikh Abdul al-Ibaba.

(The SHEIKH, wearing a traditional white robe and headress, crosses to CANDOO.)

CANDOO

Welcome to the Acropolis, Sheikh *(pronounced "sheek.")*

SHEIKH

(Correcting him.)

Sheikh *(pronounced "shake.")*

CANDOO

Right, put 'er there pardner.

(CANDOO grabs the SHEIKH's hand and pumps it vigorously.)

I am greatly honored by your visit.

SHEIKH

It is I who am honored.

CANDOO

The honor is mine.

SHEIKH

No one can have more honor than Sheikh Abdul-bin-Mohammed al-Ibaba.

CANDOO

Except me, A.J. Jones, President and Chief Executive Officer of Candooco, Incorporated.

SHEIKH

Okay, you take the honor and I'll have a drink. My cousin the King is a very religious man. He requires that the royal family obey the rules of the Koran, which allow us four wives but forbids the consumption of alcohol. With one wife, perhaps you do not need alcohol, but with four wives you need much to drink, very much to drink.

CANDOO

What can I get you?

SHEIKH

A martini, with a pinch of sand. I like it very dry.

CANDOO

Marbury, there's some gin in my tent. And get Gloria to come here. I want her to meet our distinguished guest.

(*MARBURY exits.*)

Sheikh, you know this is the Parthenon, the great temple built by the ancient Greeks to show the world they were so rich and powerful they could spend a fortune on a bunch of useless buildings and still dominate everyone around them. It must have been really somethin' when it was new, and it's still pretty impressive when you consider how old it is.

SHEIKH

Yes, yes, very impressive.

CANDOO

The Greeks have never had enough money to fix it up into a really nice place, but I'm goin' to do somethin' about that.

SHEIKH

You could make it into a shrine like our Mecca and have people come from all over to worship here.

CANDOO

Do you collect money from these people?

SHEIKH

Oh no, it is a holy site where all true Muslims must come to honor Mohammed at least once in their lifetimes.

CANDOO

I can't let people come here for free. It's got to be a profit center, a big profit center for my company.

SHEIKH

Let me tell you about my country. Thanks be to Allah, it is blessed with vast reserves of oil. When your brilliant engineers invented an engine that thirsts for oil as men lust for women, my country was able to satisfy that thirst.

(MARBURY enters carrying a tray with a pitcher of martinis and pours out a glass for the SHEIKH. He hands CANDOO a can of beer.)

But Allah, wise and generous in all other ways, made Saudi Arabia a desert, and thus it is difficult for us to satisfy our thirst, our very great thirst.

(He downs his drink. MARBURY refills it. GLORIA enters.)

CANDOO

Sheikh, I'd like you to meet my sister.

SHEIKH

Your sister?

CANDOO

She is unmarried and worth her weight in gold.

SHEIKH

Ah, very nice. Please have her join us. I recommend to you a martini. These are excellent.

(GLORIA starts to respond.)

CANDOO

She doesn't drink this early in the day.

SHEIKH

As I was saying, we need water for our growing population and to achieve our ambitious plans for development. Our need for water is as great as your need for oil.

(He empties his glass and chews on the sand)

The taste of sand always makes me thirsty.

21

(MARBURY refills his glass which he downs immediately.)

I understand you can bring us icebergs from the South Pole.

CANDOO

No one knows how to move an iceberg.

SHEIKH

There must be a way and you are the man who can do it.

CANDOO

They will melt before they ever get to Saudi Arabia.

SHEIKH

I hear there's an MIT professor who's invented a plastic coating that will keep them from melting.

CANDOO

It will cost millions of dollars, tens of millions.

SHEIKH

We will pay you whatever it costs.

CANDOO

We'll look into it.

SHEIKH

Our thirst is great, and you are the only one who can satisfy it.

(MARBURY fills his glass. The SHEIKH salutes GLORIA.)

SHEIKH

Here's to your lovely sister. What is her name?

CANDOO

Gloria.

SHEIKH

Gloria, you must come and visit me in Saudi Arabia.

GLORIA

And wrap myself up in all those lousy robes. No thanks.

SHEIKH

Did anyone ever tell you have beautiful eyes?

(He rises and staggers to her.)

Even with your face covered with a veil, your eyes would shine with a radiant glow.

(He leans down and kisses her hand. He sniffs up her arm.)

That smell, most unusual.

GLORIA

You like it? I had it created especially for me.

(The SHEIKH keeps sniffing, drops to the ground and sniffs some more.)

SHEIKH

It is very familiar. Very familiar.

(Everyone sniffs.)

Down here.

MARBURY

I don't smell anything.

SHEIKH

Oil! It's oil.

ARTHUR

Oil?

SHEIKH

I can smell it no matter where it is

ARTHUR

Oil under the Acropolis? Impossible.

CANDOO

He's drunk. Don't pay any attention to him.

(The SHEIKH tries to get up, grasps GLORIA'S arms and has her lift him to his feet.)

SHEIKH

Gloria, you must come to Riyadh. I make you a princess.

CANDOO

Here's your chance, Sis.

SHEIKH

With all this oil under the Acropolis, you will be rich, very rich.

(He embraces GLORIA.)

Your eyes, my sweet, they are like bottomless pools of...

GLORIA

Oil.

SHEIKH

Sparkling jewels.

(He tries to kiss her. They stumble back and fall to the ground.)

GLORIA

Help! Get this lug off of me.

SHEIKH

So round, so soft, so luscious.

(CANDOO crosses and pulls the SHEIKH off of her.)

CANDOO

That's enough, Sheikh. She's lookin' for a prince, but I reckon you're not her type.

ARTHUR

What about the icebergs?

CANDOO

Come on, Marbury, let's get him out of here.

(CANDOO and MARBURY roll the SHEIKH offstage right.)

ARTHUR

The icebergs, Pop. He was ready to go for the iceberg deal.

CANDOO

How many times do I have to tell you. I'm an oil man.

ARTHUR

But there's no oil here.

CANDOO

The Sheikh thinks there is.

ARTHUR

The Sheikh? He's crazy.

CANDOO

You can be crazy and still be right.

ARTHUR

What are you saying, that there is oil under the Acropolis?

CANDOO

Everybody is so busy lookin' at these buildings up here they don't notice the rocks holdin' them up. An oil guy like me comes along and right away sees that this is a classic salt dome. All this time, the Greeks had a fortune right here under their feet and didn't know it.

ARTHUR

How do you know? You can't be sure until you start drilling.

CANDOO

When it comes to wildcattin' oil, I've never been wrong.

ARTHUR

They're not going to let you drill here, right under the Parthenon.

CANDOO

I own this hill lock, stock, and all the barrels of oil I can pump out of it. And nobody's goin' to stop me.

> (He ascends the steps and enters the temple. GLORIA exits
> left.)

ARTHUR

He's really gone clean off his rocker. I majored in geology before I went to business school, and I can tell you there's no oil here. We've got to find a way to get rid of the Acropolis and invest in something that'll generate some income and profits.

MARBURY

Why don't we sell it to the Saudis? If they believe there's oil here, they should be willing to buy it for a very good price.

ARTHUR

They've already got more oil than anybody else, and besides we can't let this great seat of Western civilization fall into the hands of a bunch of Arabs.

MARBURY

Maybe the United Nations...

ARTHUR

The UN? God no, we don't want those guys coming in and telling us what to do. This is strictly a private matter.

MARBURY

What can you do?

ARTHUR

Somehow remove him from office and then I take over the company.

MARBURY

But he owns most of the shares.

ARTHUR

There's the Board of Directors.

MARBURY

They're all indebted to him for making them rich.

ARTHUR

Some really big company could buy us out.

MARBURY

They'd put their own man in charge, not an inexperienced guy like you.

ARTHUR

I may be young, but I've got a lot of great ideas.

(GLORIA enters.)

GLORIA

Well boys, why don't you get Geronimo to toss him off onto one of these rocks. But his head is so thick it probably wouldn't faze him.

ARTHUR

We were just kicking around some ideas about how to maximize our investments.

GLORIA

And in the process remove your father as head of the company.

ARTHUR

He's been very successful but now we need to broaden our vision beyond just the oil business. There are so many opportunities waiting for us all around the world.

GLORIA

Like this loony business with the icebergs.

ARTHUR

It's not loony. It's a sure thing, and we use the Saudi's money to finance it.

GLORIA

How do you get them through the Suez Canal?

ARTHUR

The Suez Canal?

GLORIA

You hadn't thought of that, had you?

ARTHUR

The engineers will figure it out.

MARBURY

Don't you know your geography? They won't have to go anywhere near the Suez Canal.

GLORIA

I've got a little favor to ask. I want you to find the most eligible bachelor in Europe and have him come here so I can meet him.

ARTHUR

The most eligible bachelor in Europe? We don't have time to do that.

GLORIA

You can make time.

ARTHUR

We've got a lot more important things to do.

GLORIA

What do you think will happen if I tell your father that you're plotting to depose him and take over the company?

ARTHUR

You know he's lost his grip. His mind is not focused on the business.

MARBURY

Arthur is just looking for a way to make Candooco into a broader and stronger company.

GLORIA

So Marbury, you're in on this too.

MARBURY

No, no, Candoo is still the boss as far as I'm concerned.

ARTHUR

This European, what kind of man are you looking for?

GLORIA

You tell him I'm an attractive, intelligent American woman who is seeking a cultured and sophisticated gentleman to show me the glorious wonders of Europe and to share a life of passion and pleasure.

ARTHUR

What if he wants to see a picture of you?

GLORIA

Just tell him I live on the Acropolis. He'll know right away that I have significant financial resources and am a woman who appreciates beauty and the finer things in life.

MARBURY

You don't care what nationality he is?

GLORIA

It's what he says and knows, not in what language he says it that is important.

ARTHUR

This is a pretty tough assignment. It'll take a while.

GLORIA

I want him here as soon as we get the place fixed up.

MARBURY

Gloria, you're a fine, genuine good-hearted woman from Texas. You don't need some phony European fop who's only interested in your money.

GLORIA

Marbury, I'm a much more complex person than you imagine, full of desires and talents and now it's time to open up and let them soar.

ARTHUR

Europeans don't drink bourbon. You'll have to switch to wine.

GLORIA

If I find the right man, I won't need to drink anything.

(She exits left.)

ARTHUR

Do you really think she'll tell my father?

MARBURY

If she does, he'll ship you back to Texas and that'll be the end of your career.

ARTHUR

Bitch.

(He exits left. MARBURY crosses right.)

MARBURY

Down inside she's a very simple wonderful person. If she would only recognize that and stop pretending...

(He exits. CANDOO enters talking on his cell phone.)

CANDOO

Mabel, I told you to call at night when it's cheaper. It's Sunday? Christ, I've lost all track of time. No, we don't have it fixed up yet. Got a lot of things to do first.

(ELENA enters.)

It's not at all like Texas. You wouldn't like it here. It's hottern hell. There aren't any trees, not even any grass. The food's greasy. The wine's bitter. The people don't speak English. Nobody plays bridge. It just isn't the place for you. Yeah, I will. Arthur? He's fine. I'll tell him. Did you make the arrangements about the money? Great. All for now. You too.

ELENA

I hear you speak. You do not like our country?

CANDOO

That was my wife. I was telling her she wouldn't like it over here.

ELENA

Your wife?

CANDOO

She's still back in Texas, where I think she should stay.

ELENA

A man and his wife, they should be together..

CANDOO

Look, I'm getting damned tired of you telling me what I should do.

ELENA

What I say is meant to save you from the anger of the gods.

CANDOO

I can take care of myself thanks.

ELENA

You are a barbarian unfamiliar with the way of the gods. Their wrath can be terrible to behold.

CANDOO

If they're so all powerful, how come they didn't know there's a huge pool of oil right here under the Acropolis?

ELENA

Oil? We have no need for it. We had a glorious civilization without it.

CANDOO

But think how much better you could have lived if you had learned how to harness its power.

ELENA

We believe that material wealth distracts people from pursuing what is truly important. One should at all times strive to achieve a high level of knowledge, understanding, and wisdom.

CANDOO

That's okay if you can sit around all day and don't have to work. But most people don't have that luxury. They have to produce something someone else wants and is willing to pay for. It takes a lot of power to run such a society and to have power you gotta have oil and lots of it. People have to drive and driving gives them mobility and a great sense of freedom.

ELENA

We were free and had no need to go anywhere. Everything that is required for a full and rich life was right here.

CANDOO

You don't have national parks, Disneylands, gambling casinos, and Nascar races that you have to drive to see.

ELENA

We had Olympic Games, epic dramas, beautiful art, and these magnificent temples to inspire us.

CANDOO

You need something for the average guy, football, baseball, basketball, some wild places where he can go huntin' and fishin'.

ELENA

Our citizens were serious and educated. They would not have been interested in such trivial distractions.

CANDOO

Sure, they were free to do nothin' because you had slaves to do all the work.

ELENA

And your workers, are they not shackled to their jobs as if they were slaves?

CANDOO

In America, if they work hard they can rise to be the boss and their boss's boss. It is the golden land of opportunity. There's no limit to how high people can go. Just look at me a poor boy who's made good.

ELENA

But what good is all your wealth when you are ignorant of what the greatest thinkers have thought and said?

CANDOO

I employ thousands of men and women and pay them enough to support their families and enable them to live better than anyone else in the world, and I find oil where no one else can and provide millions of people with the means to enjoy a life of great comfort and freedom.

ELENA

You allow women to work along with the men?

CANDOO

Sure. They can't do the heavy stuff, but we couldn't run the company without them.

ELENA

They should be home taking care of the children.

CANDOO

They can if they want to, but lots of them have to work and lots want to have a career just like the men.

ELENA

Our women are in charge of the home. They know little beyond how to take care of their families.

CANDOO

We give them a good education. They go to college and compete with men in almost every field.

ELENA

Women are different from men. We do not have their strength of their intelligence. We need for them to provide for us and protect us.

CANDOO

That's a lot of baloney. The governor of my state of Texas a little while ago was a woman.

ELENA

Texas?

CANDOO

It's the biggest state in America. Well it was till Alaska was admitted, but Alaska is nothin' but a whole lot of ice and Eskimos.

ELENA

I do not know much of the world beyond Greece.

CANDOO

Didn't they teach you anything in school?

ELENA

Since girls were thought never to need such knowledge, we were given instruction only in how to be good wives and mothers.

CANDOO

That's terrible. No wonder Greece didn't last very long. I can see you've got a lot of catchin' up to do. I've got to go to work, but come back and we'll start teachin' you some of the things you outta know.

(CANDOO enters the temple. ELENA exits right. ARTHUR and MARBURY enter left.)

ARTHUR

My plan seems to be working. I sent word out that the Acropolis is for sale. Everyone knows that Candoo claims there's oil under this hill, so we should be hearing from a lot of people interested in buying it.

MARBURY

There may be no oil here at all.

ARTHUR

Candoo has such a reputation for always being right that someone is sure to give us a bid. It so happens that we have a potential buyer on the way up right now.

MARBURY

Who's that?

ARTHUR

The Presidente of Paragonia.

MARBURY

Paragonia? Where in the world is Paragonia?

ARTHUR

It's one of those little countries in Latin America that are loaded with natural resources – mainly copper – that China is buying up as fast as it can.

(ARTHUR climbs the stairs and calls into the temple.)

Hey Pop, come here. We've got another visitor.

CANDOO

(From inside.)

I'm busy.

ARTHUR

It's important. Very important.

CANDOO

Who is it?

ARTHUR

The Presidente of Paragonia.

CANDOO

Paragonia? Never heard of it.

ARTHUR

It's a country in Latin America that has gotten rich from selling copper to the Chinese.

CANDOO

(*Emerging from the temple.*)

I don't need any copper.

ARTHUR

He wants to talk about oil. He needs oil to develop his growing economy.

(*THE PRESIDENTE OF PARAGONIA enters from the left. He is a small man wearing an ornate uniform, festooned with many metals, that is too large for him. He is wearing a black armband, an oversize military hat, and a sword that drags the ground.*)

CANDOO

Howdy, Mister Presidente. Welcome to the Acropolis. Mighty nice of you to drop in on us.

PRESIDENTE

I know the Greeks were bankrupt, but I deed not theenk they would let eet go to rueen like thees.

CANDOO

We still have a lot of fixin' up to do. How was your trip?

PRESIDENTE

I have just been to Sweetzerland. It ees wonderful country, don't you theenk?

CANDOO

Bein' from Texas, all those mountains make me dizzy.

PRESIDENTE

I don't mean the mountains. I mean the <u>banks</u>. They take the money and don't ask any questions.

CANDOO

I don't keep much money in a bank. I put it to work back in my company so it can keep on growin'.

PRESIDENTE

You leeve in Paragonia, you get your money out of the country real queek. The peeble, they want to have democracy, elections to choose some stupid communeest to run the country.

CANDOO

You still have communists in Paragonia?

PRESIDENTE

We shoot most of them, but in a republica you cannot shoot everybody.

CANDOO

(Laughing.)

You gotta leave someone to vote for you.

PRESIDENTE

One hundred per cent. They make me Presidente for Life. That ees problem. Many peeble want to make me dead.

CANDOO

That armband you're wearing, did someone die?

PRESIDENTE

Yes, my wife.

CANDOO

I'm sorry.

PRESIDENTE

No need. I keel her.

CANDOO

You killed her?

PRESIDENTE

She was a whore.

CANDOO

You kill a woman for that?

PRESIDENTE

She had a lover, a miner, she want to make Presidente.

CANDOO

A much younger man?

PRESIDENTE

A miner, a man who deeg for copper.

CANDOO

What can I do for you?

PRESIDENTE

I have a proposeetion.

CANDOO

Okay, shoot.

PRESIDENTE

You geeve me the Acropolis, and I geeve you Paragonia.

CANDOO

What?

PRESIDENTE

Eet is fair trade, no?

CANDOO

Paragonia for the Acropolis?

PRESIDENTE

My country is reech in resources – copper, tin, zinc, marijuana, poppies...

CANDOO

If it's got all that, how come you want to give it away?

PRESIDENTE

The peeble are restless. They are unhappy. They want democracy. They are too stupid to know they are better off under me, the Presidente for Life.

CANDOO

Why don't you educate them and develop your economy so there are plenty of jobs and then they'd keep you in power.

PRESIDENTE

I try, but there ees nobody to teach them.

CANDOO

There are plenty of countries who'd be willing to send skilled teachers to get things started.

PRESIDENTE

You do not understand my country. The peeble they do not trust foreigners who take everytheeng out of my country and geeve nothing back to the peeble. That is why we are so poor.

CANDOO

There must be a way to get your country started on the road to prosperity.

PRESIDENTE

Yes, and you are the one who can do eet.

CANDOO

I'm just a simple businessman. I don't know anything about running a country.

ARTHUR

Pop, here's one way to diversify into a whole new line of industries. It's just what we need.

CANDOO

My son went to business school where they teach you everything but common sense.

PRESIDENTE

I cannot go back to Paragonia. They weel keel me.

CANDOO

Tell you what, we'll let you stay here if you marry my sister.

PRESIDENTE

Your seester?

MARBURY

Candoo, no.

CANDOO

She's rich and she's a virgin.

PRESIDENTE

You mean no one...

CANDOO

Si.

PRESIDENTE

Olé.

CANDOO

(With a mischievous smile.)

That's the idea.

PRESIDENTE

Where ees she?

CANDOO

Gloria. Gloria, there's a man here who wants to meet you.

(GLORIA emerges from her tent.)

GLORIA

You want me?

CANDOO

This gentleman says he would like to meet you.

(The PRESIDENTE backs off, shocked at her size.)

PRESIDENTE

Senorita, you are...you are lovely, you are beautiful. You take my breath away. Your brother, what he tells me about you makes my blood to boil, my heart to burn.

GLORIA

Who is this guy?

PRESIDENTE

I gaze into your eyes and see a woman who has been waiting all her life for a man like me, José Luis Gomez y Gomez, the Presidente for Life of the Republica of Paragonia.

GLORIA

Para-what?

PRESIDENTE

Paragonia, the copper capital of Lateen America.

GLORIA

Arty, is this some kind of joke?

PRESIDENTE

I am madly in love weeth you. Let me geeve you a kees and you weel feel the fire of my passion for you.

(He lunges for her. GLORIA backs away. The PRESIDENTE'S pants, which are several sizes too big for him, fall down around his feet. He draws his sword, pins his pants to the ground, and steps out of them. He waves his sword like a phallus at GLORIA.)

GLORIA

For Christ's sake, somebody stop him.

(MARBURY steps forward. The PRESIDENTE swings his sword at him causing MARBURY to fall over a chunk of

*marble. ARTHUR grabs the PRESIDENTE'S arm and
wrenches the sword away. He picks up the PRESIDENTE'S
pants and hustles the PRESIDENTE offstage right.)*

GLORIA

Arty, you bastard.

CANDOO

You say you want some foreigner to take you as far away from Texas as
possible.

GLORIA

I don't mean a sleezy scumbag like that.

CANDOO

You know these Latin Americans, they do get overly excited.

(MARBURY, lying on the ground, moans.)

GLORIA

Marbury, are you all right?

MARBURY

I think so.

GLORIA

Your head. You've got a cut on your head.

*(She dabs the wound with her handkerchief. CANDOO
exits.)*

It's not bad, just a scratch.

MARBURY

(Taking her hand.)

Thanks.

GLORIA

I hope we don't get any more dirty old men like that.

MARBURY

The oil will attract a lot of unsavory characters I'm afraid.

GLORIA

Aren't there any really nice men in the oil business?

MARBURY

There are some, but they're all back in Texas. Neither one of us should have ever left the good old US of A.

GLORIA

I don't know. There must be another Charles Boyer somewhere over here.

(She takes his arm and leads him offstage right. CANDOO emerges from the temple, descends the steps and enters the portable toilet. ELENA appears left. CANDOO steps out and starts to zip up his fly. Seeing ELENA, he turns his back and finishes the zip.)

CANDOO

What the hell. Can't a man have any privacy around here?

ELENA

I have come because. .you said you could teach me things I should know.

CANDOO

Yes.

ELENA

To you, I must appear to be very ignorant.

CANDOO

You seem to be intelligent. You just haven't had any schoolin'

ELENA

It is true, but now I wish to learn.

CANDOO

There's so much, it's hard to know where to start.

ELENA

With something simple perhaps.

CANDOO

Well they say it all began with the Big Bang.

ELENA

The Big Bang?

CANDOO

The universe, it was once a little ball that exploded in what scientists call the Big Bang.

ELENA

The universe?

CANDOO

The sky, all the stuff that's out there, the stars, the galaxies.

ELENA

The stars, they are so beautiful, on a dark night.

CANDOO

The weird thing is, they're all movin' away from us.

ELENA

If that is so, they should be getting smaller, shouldn't they?

CANDOO

They're so far away, you don't notice it.

ELENA

I do not understand.

CANDOO

You want to know the truth, I don't either. But that's what they tell us, and I guess they know what they're talkin' about .

ELENA

You believe things you do not understand?

CANDOO

All the guys who study these things seem to agree.

ELENA

We believe the gods fixed the stars in the sky.

CANDOO

The gods?

ELENA

That is what we are told.

CANDOO

That's ridiculous. They're billions of miles away and hottern hell.

ELENA

The gods are all-knowing and have been around for a long time, in fact forever.

CANDOO

From what I've heard, they're cruel and horny, much like us except they never die.

ELENA

It is a very dull and boring life.

CANDOO

You don't get old, you live forever, sounds great to me.

ELENA

It's the same thing day after day. There's no joy, nothing to stir the blood or thrill the heart, no one to share your pleasures or brighten your sadness, nothing to look forward to, for tomorrow will be the same as today and yesterday and the day before that.

CANDOO

There must be some way to have some fun.

ELENA

The gods enjoy playing dirty tricks on mortals, and even on one another, just to relieve their boredom. They cannot show affection for anyone because then they would be bound to that person.

CANDOO

Is that so bad?

ELENA

Do you know what it would be like to be bound forever to someone you come to hate?

CANDOO

Yeah, I see what you mean.

ELENA

It is a very hard and lonely life.

CANDOO

If you could find someone to love, it would be a lot better.

ELENA

Love? I know the word, but I know not what it is like.

(Voices offstage.)

CANDOO

Someone's coming. Come back when you can.

(ELENA exits. ARTHUR rushes in.)

ARTHUR

Pop, we've got a visitor.

CANDOO

Not now, I'm busy.

ARTHUR

He's very important.

CANDOO

I said I'm busy.

ARTHUR

It's the Prime Minister of Japan.

CANDOO

What does he want?

ARTHUR

He says he'll only speak to you.

CANDOO

The Prime Minister of Japan?

ARTHUR

It must be very important.

CANDOO

It's just as I predicted. We buy the Acropolis and the VIP's from all over start coming here to pay their respects.

(ARTHUR leaves and returns with the PRIME MINISTER, dressed in a business suit, who bows and moves forward, forcing CANDOO up the steps. MARBURY and GLORIA enter.)

PRIME MINISTER

I bring greetings from all people of Japan. We very grateful for what your country give to my country – peace, democracy, free-enterprise system, and can-do spirit. Japanese work very hard, productivity very high because we know we can do anything if we try hard.

CANDOO

You're damn right. Here's a man after my own heart.

PRIME MINISTER

We rike do business with your company. Can be very profible for us both.

CANDOO

Right again. Who said you fellows were hard to get along with.

PRIME MINISTER

We rike buy Acroporis.

CANDOO

Buy the Acropolis?

PRIME MINISTER

You need money. We need oil. Very good we make deal.

CANDOO

I can't sell the Acropolis to you. It's one of the great monuments of Western civilization.

MARBURY

It's against the law to discriminate on the basis of race.

CANDOO

Bullshit Marbury. Over here I can do anything I damned well don't want to.

PRIME MINISTER

We have much yen for Acroporis, 4 trillion yen.

CANDOO

It's not for sale.

MARBURY

That's nearly 50 billion dollars.

PRIME MINISTER

Japan must have oil or Japan die. What price you want?

CANDOO

It's not for sale at any price. Can't you understand simple English?

PRIME MINISTER

(Bowing.)

So solly.

(He continues to bow as he backs off to the right.)

Sayonara. Have nice day.

(He exits and immediately a SAMURAI enters. He is wearing the costume of a medieval warrior. His hand on his sword, he stomps across the stage, grunting Japanese in a coarse, menacing voice. He bows and pulls out his sword with the stylized movement that has taken him years to master.)

MARBURY

I knew we should have sold it to them. Now they're going to take it by force.

CANDOO

Like hell they are.

(The SAMURAI bows again. CANDOO descends the steps and extends his hand. Confused, the SAMURAI steps back and bows again. Hand outstretched, CANDOO grabs the SAMURAI'S sword arm and throws him to the ground. The SAMURAI scrambles to his feet, recovers his sword, and prepares to charge. CANDOO leans down and picks up a long rope with a lasso at the end. When the SAMURAI charges, CANDOO swings the rope at him causing the SAMURAI to duck and fall over a

chunk of marble. CANDOO climbs the steps, turns, and throws the lasso over the SAMURAI'S head as he regains his feet. The rope drops to the SAMURAI'S waist. CANDOO pulls it tight, pinning the SAMURAI'S arms to his side.)

CANDOO

The Acropolis is mine and goin' to stay mine. I don't guess you know English but you get the message, okay mister.

(CANDOO hands the rope to ARTHUR, who pulls the SAMURAI offstage right. GLORIA picks up his sword and follows behind. CANDOO mounts the steps to the magisterial music of Beethoven's Eroica Symphony. At the top, he adopts an imperious pose as he gazes out over the scene below. MARBURY steps forward.)

MARBURY

Candoo.

(No response.)

Candoo.

(No response.)

Mr. President.

CANDOO

(In an imperial voice maintained throughout this scene.)

Yes.

MARBURY

Since you intend to keep title to the Acropolis in perpetuity, you really must write a will. You can't put it off any longer.

CANDOO

Why not?

MARBURY

For a man of your means, it's completely irresponsible to die intestate.

CANDOO

My private parts are nobody's business but my own.

MARBURY

"Intestate" simply means "without a will." Only if you write a will can you be sure your intentions will be carried out.

CANDOO

And if I don't die, I don't need a will, right?

MARBURY

I suppose not. I mean of course you need a will. Everyone dies——eventually.

CANDOO

I've decided not to.

MARBURY

What?

CANDOO

It's all a matter of will power. If I will I will not die, I will live and will not need a will.

MARBURY

Remember the old saying about death and taxes.

CANDOO

You've arranged it so I don't pay any taxes. I'll arrange it so I don't die.

MARBURY

That's impossible.

CANDOO

Nothing's impossible

MARBURY

No one's ever managed to escape death.

CANDOO

Christ did.

MARBURY

But he was the son of God. He was divine.

CANDOO

I'm divine as far as I'm concerned.

> (*The Eroica Symphony resumes. MARBURY falls back in wonder.*)

END OF ACT I

ACT II

The set is the same as in ACT I. ARTHUR and MARBURY enter right.

ARTHUR

He says he wants to drill as soon as he can get some rigs up here.

MARBURY

He's passed up every opportunity to unload the Acropolis without having to drill a single hole.

ARTHUR

We've got to do something before he does anything really crazy.

MARBURY

He's already crazy. Anyone who refuses to write a will is nuts.

ARTHUR

That's it! Of course. We get him committed.

MARBURY

You can't put a man away for not writing a will, unfortunately.

ARTHUR

Didn't he claim he's divine?

MARBURY

Yes.

ARTHUR

Then no problem. They lock up people just for claiming they're Teddy Roosevelt charging up San Juan Hill.

MARBURY

How do you do it?

ARTHUR

What do you think psychiatrists are for?

MARBURY

To keep you so broke you can't get into any real trouble.

ARTHUR

I get one to declare him insane and pack him off to a nice asylum somewhere. And then I become the President and Chief Executive Officer of Candooco.

(They exit right, CANDOO enters left talking on his cell phone.)

CANDOO

Look Mabel, I can't come home right now. I'm in the middle of some very important business. Oil? Under the Acropolis. Where did you hear that? Well yes, I think there is. I <u>know</u> there is. That's why I bought this place. We'll be drilling soon.

(ELENA appears.)

With our new technology, we won't damage anything up here, but it will be kind of a mess for a while. I know, I know, you need someone to escort you to the big gala at the Club. Get your old pal Billy Bob to take you. You know how he loves to be seen with the most beautiful women in Houston. As soon as I get the rigs set up. Arthur? He's fine. Yeah, I'll tell him. You too.

(He hangs up. ELENA steps forward.)

ELENA

Your wife. She must be very lonely with you away for so long.

CANDOO

She's used to it. I'm on the road a lot. She can brag to all her friends about my ownin' the Acropolis. That'll impress all those snobs in Houston. None of them's got anythin' like what I've got here.

ELENA

Do you love your wife?

CANDOO

Love my wife? Of course. I'm married to her.

ELENA

What is love like?

CANDOO

What is it like?

ELENA

What do you do with her?

CANDOO

Do with her?

ELENA

Do you talk to her, share your joys and your frustrations, tell her why you need her?

CANDOO

We talk, yeah, we talk about…about what to do with the money, what she wants to do with the money. Buy a bigger house, a fancier car, another fur coat.

ELENA

Do you like to do things for her, to be with her?

CANDOO

We're both real busy. She's got her garden club, her bridge club, her golf club, her charities.

ELENA

Charities?

CANDOO

Those are groups devoted to saving the whales, the trees, the Alamo, the starving kids in Africa, Armenia, and god knows where else.

ELENA

She must have had to spend a great deal of time with her children.

CANDOO

We have only one, a son, who's here with me now. When he was little, we had a nanny to take care of him.

ELENA

A nanny?

CANDOO

Kind of like a maid.

ELENA

We sometimes had slaves to help with the children, but it was the mother's main responsibility. Husbands spent the day away managing the government and the commerce required to keep Athens strong and prosperous, activities the women were not to be concerned with.

CANDOO

A lot of American women work and some have been very successful, but Mabel doesn't know anything about business and doesn't want to know anything about the oil business. She thinks it's all rather crude.

That's supposed to be funny. The word "crude" is another word for oil and it also means coarse and vulgar.

ELENA

Crude.

CANDOO

It's a play on words. She's saying the oil business is rough and dirty.

ELENA

Since you are in the oil business, she thinks you are crude.

CANDOO

You got it.

(ELENA *breaks into a smile.*)

You know, you're very pretty when you smile.

ELENA

I come again to warn you that your arrogance is greatly displeasing to the gods and that they forbid you to remove anything from under the Acropolis. This hill is sacred to the soul of Greece and must not be desecrated in any way.

CANDOO

You can go tell your gods wherever they are to stay the hell out of my way.

ELENA

For the last time, if you challenge the gods, Zeus himself will come down from Olympus and destroy you.

CANDOO

Zeus?

ELENA

The father of the gods and the most powerful one of them all.

CANDOO

He better not mess with me, A.J. "Candoo" Jones or he'll be very sorry.

(ELENA exits right. MARBURY enters carrying a briefcase.)

MARBURY

I thought I heard you talking to somebody.

CANDOO

Oh yeah, my wife. She keeps wantin' to know when I'm comin' home.

MARBURY

You know how I feel about that. We never should have come here in the first place.

CANDOO

We're in the oil business Marbury. That means you go find and drill for it wherever it is.

MARBURY

There are lots of other places where the prospects are very promising.

CANDOO

You would rather be in Siberia?

MARBURY

I just don't like the idea of tearing up the Acropolis. It is a sacred hill, not only to the Greeks but to the whole world.

CANDOO

We're not goin' to tear up the Acropolis. We extract the oil, fix up the place so it's better than we found it, and sell it back to the Greeks.

(CANDOO exits. MARBURY sits and pulls some papers from his briefcase. GLORIA enters carrying a glass of bourbon.)

GLORIA

You've always got your nose in some of those stupid papers. You're supposed to be finding me a nice cultured European gentleman.

MARBURY

Candoo is about to start drilling. No gentleman's about to come here when it's littered with oil rigs.

GLORIA

Marbury, this is my last chance. I've got to find someone. I can't go back to Texas alone, I just can't.

(She sits beside him and starts to cry. He gives her his handkerchief.)

MARBURY

You're a wonderful person Gloria. You need someone who appreciates all the splendid qualities you have but keep hidden behind the false facade you present to the public that's not the real you.

GLORIA

I'm just a big fat slob who nobody's ever going to love.

MARBURY

That's not true.

> (He takes her hand, starts raising it to his lips when an intruder stumbles in from the right. It is ZEUS. Wearing a faded purple toga, he is carrying his thunderbolt and a wineskin slung over his shoulder. Although possessed of a rope-coiled beard and a crown of olive leaves, he does not have the commanding presence of a god but the furtive appearance of a bum down on his luck. He holds up the wineskin and squeezes a stream into his mouth. Lifting the skin once more, he squirts out the last few drops, some of which fall onto his foot. Steadying himself with his thunderbolt, he leans down, swipes them up with his finger, and licks them off with his tongue. Gazing about, he sees MARBURY and GLORIA.)

ZEUS

Wine, I need some wine. Have you some of the noble juice you can share with me?

> (He squeezes the wineskin.)

This is dry as a hag's tit.

MARBURY

Who are you?

ZEUS

I have come to tell you, to tell you to desist in your barbarous ways and to leave this hill forthwith, that is quickly and right now.

GLORIA

How did this bum get up here?

ZEUS

Your arrogance has gone to the extreme of hubris, you have violated our most important rule and arrogated to yourself the power of the gods. This cannot be allowed.

GLORIA

What's he talking about?

MARBURY

I believe you are speaking to the wrong person.

ZEUS

You are not the barbarian who claims to be king of the Acropolis?

MARBURY

No.

ZEUS

Then take me to him. But first give me some wine. My thirst is an aching that gives me no peace.

GLORIA

We don't have any wine but here's a glass of bourbon

ZEUS

Bur-bon?

GLORIA

It'll mellow all your problems.

(ZEUS drinks, gasps, and cries out.)

ZEUS

Aargh! It burns like fire.

GLORIA

You get used to it, you'll like it.

ZEUS

Water, I need water.

(MARBURY hands him a small bottle of water. CANDOO emerges from the temple.)

CANDOO

What's goin' on out here?

MARBURY

This guy wants to talk to you.

CANDOO

Who is he?

GLORIA

Some wino who somehow got through security.

CANDOO

Go tell 'em to come up and get him out of here.

(GLORIA and MARBURY exit.)

ZEUS

(Finishing the water bottle.)

You are the new king of the Acropolis?

CANDOO

I own it if that's what you mean.

ZEUS

Your arrogance has gone to the extreme of hubris. You have violated our most important rule.

CANDOO

Who the hell are you?

ZEUS

You have arrogated to yourself the power of the gods.

CANDOO

Damn right. And what are you goin' to do about it?

ZEUS

This cannot be allowed.

CANDOO

Says who?

ZEUS

I speak for all the gods.

CANDOO

So you are Mr. Zeus, the biggest one they've got?

ZEUS

Do not be deceived. My power is awesome. I can move mountains and roil the seas. I can ravage the land and destroy those who oppose my will. I am the king of the gods. Before me and my thunderbolt all men quake with fear. Or once they did. But now my life is a misery. Mt. Olympus is a cauldron of frustration and bitterness. Aphrodite roams the palace complaining that she has no lovers, Artemis that she has nothing to hunt, Ares that he has no wars to fight, Hermes that he has no messages to deliver. No one requires Hephaestus at the forge. The sun rises and sets with no help from Apollo. It is an asylum of the powerless. The only thing they can do is talk, and talk they do, all day and on through the night, about the days when they reigned supreme and were feared and revered by all mortals here on earth. They blame me for not regaining dominion over those who once worshiped us. The only way I can endure their incessant nagging is to drown out their voices with this (he holds up the wineskin). When Hera wishes to torture me with their rantings, she locks up the wine, and I have to leave Olympus to keep from going mad.

CANDOO

You poor guy. That's really a sad story.

ZEUS

Some wine. Would you have some wine? My head is pounding with a thousand hammers.

CANDOO

I've got no wine but I'll give you some advice. You want to be treated like a god, you gotta act like a god. First thing you do is stop feeling sorry for yourself. Sure you're in a tough situation. That happens to everyone. But you gotta forget about that. Look at the positive side. You're not crippled or sick or stupid or senile. You got a lot goin' for you. You start by setting some goals, not easy ones but ones that make you stretch, go beyond what you think you can do. As you succeed, you'll build up your confidence and go on to accomplish things you never thought you could do. After a while, you'll find that anything is possible.

ZEUS

It may work for you, but you are a barbarian.

CANDOO

It's all in your mind. Change your attitude and really believe you can do anything you set out to do, really believe it, and you'll find there's nothing beyond your reach.

ZEUS

I think like a god, I can be a god?

CANDOO

Yes.

ZEUS

I speak and men listen. I command and they obey.

CANDOO

You got it.

ZEUS

I'll send Hera down to Hades, kick Hephaestus off Olympus so he'll have to go back to work, ship my brother Poseidon back to sea where he belongs.

CANDOO

You can do it.

ZEUS

I am again Olympian Zeus, king of the gods as in the golden days of Hellas when this head gave birth to Athena, when these lungs blew savage winds out of the north, when these arms struck down all who challenged my supremacy, when these loins sired heroes and demigods and enjoyed the favors of many a beauteous woman. Ah, women—I had forgotten their manifold charms. Soft lips and swelling breasts and satin thighs. Are they as skilled in the arts of love as when last I knew them?

CANDOO

Better. They've gotten a lot more experience since then.

ZEUS

And strong? It takes a powerful woman to please a god.

CANDOO

They sure know how to take care of <u>me</u>.

ZEUS

I haven't felt this good since Alexander defeated Darius and took control of all of Persia. Where are the women?

CANDOO

Women? Well my sister is here.

ZEUS

Where is she?

CANDOO

Look around. You can't miss her.

(ZEUS exits left. CANDOO ascends the steps. ARTHUR
enters right with DR. ROWAN D. BEND, a psychiatrist who
is wearing a loud sports jacket and a pointed black beard and
is carrying a small black bag.)

ARTHUR

Pop, I'd like you to meet Dr. Bend. He's a psychiatrist here conducting a survey to find out what accounts for the success of the world's greatest men.

CANDOO

You want to know why I'm successful, I'll tell you why, and I'm sure it's the same for all the other fellows on your list.

DR. BEND

That's very interesting. My theory is that all successful men are alike, but each failure is a failure in his own way.

CANDOO

Damn right. Every successful man succeeds through will power. Every loser has a different excuse for his failure.

DR. BEND

(Pulling out a notebook.)

I've got to write that down.

CANDOO

What other great men are you talkin' to in this survey?

DR. BEND

Before we get into that, I need to ask you some questions.

CANDOO

Okay, shoot.

(They sit down.)

DR. BEND

Are you heterosexual, homosexual, bisexual, or something else?

CANDOO

What do you mean by something else?

DR. BEND

You'd know if you were one.

CANDOO

(To ARTHUR.)

What's he talkin' about? Have I been missin' something?

ARTHUR

I don't think so.

DR. BEND

Some people get a great deal of pleasure from pain.

CANDOO

Well not me.

DR. BEND

You don't know until you've tried it.

ARTHUR

Put down heterosexual, raging.

CANDOO

What's the matter with that?

DR. BEND

It strikes me that a man in your position might like to try something a little different.

CANDOO

Different?

(ARTHUR crosses to confer with DR. BEND.)

DR. BEND

(To CANDOO.)

I understand you claim you're not going to die.

CANDOO

Only when I'm good and ready.

DR. BEND

What makes you think that you, alone of all men, can escape the inevitability of death?

CANDOO

The reason people die is because they don't have the will to keep on livin'. Well I do and I will.

DR. BEND

You realize that defies all the laws of medicine, chemistry, and common sense. Did it ever occur to you that you might be crazy?

CANDOO

Never.

DR. BEND

You'll have to admit that you're unusual.

CANDOO

Unusual? Of course I'm unusual. I have created a business where there was none before, employed thousands of people who might otherwise be unemployed, discovered oil that would still be hidden in the ground, taken risks no one else is willing to take. I'm an entrepreneur, Doctor, and therefore too valuable to die.

DR. BEND

Do you really believe that?

CANDOO

Absolutely.

DR. BEND

Obviously an advanced case of megalomania, egomania, satyriasis with overtones of paranoia.

(He rises and ascends the steps.)

Standing here, you imagine that you have unlimited power, that you are omnipotent.

(He grows more excited with his own sense of power.)

No one dares to contradict you. No one denies you anything. Name whatever you want and it's yours.

(He claps his hands and points to ARTHUR.)

Hand me my bag.

(ARTHUR gives him the bag, from which he takes out a whip.)

From here there is nothing one cannot create, nothing one cannot destroy.

(He cracks the whip at CANDOO.)

Olaf, tie him up.

(OLAF, a man in a white suit, enters with CANDOO's lasso, binds his hands behind his back and ties him to one of the columns. CANDOO resists but to no avail.)

CANDOO

What the hell do you think you are doin'?

DR. BEND

You'll be all right. There are a number of new cures for your condition.

(He quickly removes his coat, tie, and shirt in a fever of excitement. GLORIA enters.)

GLORIA

What the hell's going on here?

(DR. BEND cracks his whip.)

DR. BEND

Ah lovely lady, come here.

GLORIA

What?

ARTHUR

Better do what he says.

(DR. BEND hands her the whip, climbs the steps and embraces one of the columns. He grinds his hips against the marble, his back exposed to GLORIA with the whip.)

GLORIA

Who is this nut?

DR. BEND

Go ahead, hit me.

(GLORIA flicks the whip across his back.)

Harder.

(GLORIA does as commanded.)

Harder!

(GLORIA draws back the whip. ZEUS enters and rushes
toward GLORIA.)

ZEUS

There you are.

(MARBURY tries to stop him. GLORIA turns to confront her
wild-eyed attacker.)

My dear, you are so…lovely.

(ZEUS breaks free from MARBURY. GLORIA swings the
whip around and cracks it at ZEUS. He stops, raises his
thunderbolt. MARBURY knocks it away. GLORIA cracks the
whip at ZEUS' ankles. He grabs his leg in pain.)

My beauty, I mean you no harm.

GLORIA

It's this dirty old bum again.

ZEUS

Tell me, who do you want me to be?

GLORIA

A gentleman, something you couldn't possibly understand.

(He approaches her. She cracks the whip. He jumps out of the way.)

Get him out of here, quick, before I crack this in his face.

(MARBURY leads ZEUS limping off right. DR. BEND has finished his orgasm against the column and is sitting on the steps. OLAF scoops up the doctor's jacket and shirt and helps the doctor into the temple.)

CANDOO

Someone come up here and untie this rope.

GLORIA

(To ARTHUR.)

What have you done to your father?

ARTHUR

It wasn't me. It was the doctor. He declared him insane and had him tied up.

CANDOO

Stop your chatter and get me loose.

ARTHUR

Sorry Pop but I'm taking over now. It was a mistake to come over here. I'm going to sell the Acropolis, and we're all going back to Texas.

CANDOO

You are like hell. I'm still the President of Candooco and I say we're staying here.

ARTHUR

(Waving some papers.)

I've got the papers right here, signed by Dr. Bend, that authorizes me to commit you. I understand there's a nice asylum in Galveston where you'll be well taken care of.

CANDOO

You dirty rotten bastard. I brought you up, sent you to a fancy school, done my best to teach you the business, and you turn around and do this.

GLORIA

Not so fast you little jerk. Neither one of you is fit to run the company as far as I can see. We'll stay here until I can find my prince charming and then you can do what you want to with this place.

(ARTHUR lunges at her. GLORIA cracks the whip.)

GLORIA

Don't mess with me Junior if you don't want to lose your balls.

ARTHUR

You're too dumb to run anything bigger than a lemonade stand.

GLORIA

You're going to be very sorry you said that.

ARTHUR

We'll see.

(He exits.)

CANDOO

Okay, now come up here and get me out of this rope.

GLORIA

Arty, you know you are an arrogant egomaniac who needs to be taken down a peg or two.

CANDOO

Get your ass up here and untie me.

GLORIA

When you learn to talk like a gentleman, I'll consider it.

(She exits. CANDOO wrestles with the rope but cannot free himself. ELENA enters.)

ELENA

I warned you that Zeus was very angry about your overweening hubris. If you challenge the gods, they will destroy you.

CANDOO

Mr. Zeus didn't do this. It was my good for nothing excuse for a son.

ELENA

But Zeus is here...

CANDOO

He arrived a drunken bum complainin' about his life on Olympus but I told him to quit bein' sorry for himself and exercise his will power to get his old power back. And it seemed to work.

ELENA

My father has not been well for a long time.

CANDOO

Your father? Zeus is your father?

ELENA

Yes, and that is why I am condemned to live forever.

CANDOO

If he gets his old strength back, maybe it will be better for you too.

ELENA

No. Nobody believes in us anymore. We are of no use to anyone and serve no worthwhile purpose.

CANDOO

There must be some Greeks somewhere who believe...

ELENA

You are blessed to be a mortal. How I envy you. You have so little time. Every moment is precious. When I rise in the morning, I say, "Today is the day." But as the sun crosses the sky, I don't seem to care. "Why today? Tomorrow is soon enough." And so it goes, year after year. Nothing is important. Nothing has any meaning.

CANDOO

Me, I'll just keep on doin' what I'm doin' now. I'll find oil where no one else can find it and make life better for millions of people.

ELENA

You'll discover that doing the same thing over and over becomes terribly boring and brings you no pleasure.

CANDOO

Then I'll try and do something different.

ELENA

That too will become boring and unsatisfying. And after you've done everything, what then?

CANDOO

That could take a while, a very long time.

ELENA

You'll find that time becomes a torture. Day after day, dum, dum, dum, dum, dum, dum – it never speeds up or slows down. It never stops. It is inexorable, implacable, a tyrant even the gods cannot escape.

CANDOO

I've overcome every obstacle in my way. I'm sure I can overcome any I'm confronted with in the future.

ELENA

The worst is having no one you need and no one who needs you.

CANDOO

There must be someone.

ELENA

We immortals only know how to hurt each other. It's our principal way of passing the time. Pain is the only emotion we can truly feel.

CANDOO

(Taking her hand.)

I'm sorry. In my world, a lovely girl like you would have many men swooning over your beauty.

ELENA

No one has ever said anything like that to me.

CANDOO

You could fill any man's life with joy and happiness.

ELENA

If only I were mortal.

CANDOO

Right now you can help me by untying this rope.

(She steps back.)

My son had this crazy psychiatrist tie me up so he could take over the company.

ELENA

Your request is something I cannot do.

CANDOO

Why not?

ELENA

Zeus has come down to punish you. It is not for me to give you your freedom.

CANDOO

Zeus has nothin' to do with this.

ELENA

He wants to see you humbled.

CANDOO

And you, is that what you want?

ELENA

What I want, no one cares what I want.

(She exits. GLORIA enters carrying a glass of bourbon.)

GLORIA

Would you like a drink Arty? It might calm you down so you can act like a gentleman.

CANDOO

Are you goin' to let me loose or be the ungrateful tub of lard you've always been?

GLORIA

That's not a very nice thing to say.

CANDOO

You'd be nothin' without me and you know it.

GLORIA

You don't look like such a big shot yourself right now.

CANDOO

I'm sendin' your ass back to Texas on the next plane.

(GLORIA mounts the steps.)

GLORIA

I think you're the one who's going to be on that plane Arty. (She raises her glass.) Right now I'm the queen of this hill.

(ZEUS enters wearing a great purple robe lined with white fur, a wide velvet plumed hat, and a black mask over his eyes. He crosses to the steps and bows to GLORIA.)

ZEUS

Your majesty.

(GLORIA does not know what to make of this magnificent figure. ZEUS pulls a rose from his robe.)

Such beauty deserves a gift to match its dazzling radiance. The fragrance of this rose represents the ardor of my affection for you that rises from the very bottom of my heart.

GLORIA

I can accept nothing from someone whom I know not.

ZEUS

It is offered by one overwhelmed by your noble countenance and queenly virtue, which shine forth like the rays of the noonday sun.

(He hands her the rose.)

GLORIA

I am flattered, sire, but the bearer of such compliments must tell me who he is truly or I cannot believe the compliments to be true.

ZEUS

As Plato once said, or perhaps it was Socrates. "Mystery is the spice of love."

GLORIA

Take off the mask. How can I trust a man whose eyes I cannot see?

ZEUS

I dare not. They will only frighten you with the intensity of my desire.

GLORIA

(Smelling the rose.)

If a mere gaze could unsettle me, my Lord, I would not be here standing on the steps of this magnificent temple.

ZEUS

(Offering her his hand.)

Then come look at them more closely.

(She hands her glass to CANDOO and descends the steps holding his hand. He puts his arm about her and sweeps her away to the tune of the Blue Danube Waltz. As they dance about the stage, she stares into his eyes. The music stops.)

GLORIA

Who are you?

ZEUS

Who would you like me to be?

GLORIA

A prince, a prince from a fair and cultured land.

ZEUS

I am the <u>king</u> of my country.

GLORIA

The king?

ZEUS

It is beautiful and the very center of civilization.

GLORIA

Yeah?

ZEUS

But a king's life is a lonely life. He needs someone to share his joys and his sorrows.

GLORIA

A woman also has such needs.

ZEUS

I can make you a queen.

GLORIA

A real queen?

ZEUS

My darling.

(He embraces her.)

Your skin is so smooth, your cheek so soft, your hair so sweet, your neck so white.

(He kisses her hungrily and leads her toward one of the tents.)

GLORIA

(Realizing she has been tricked.)

No.

ZEUS

I love you my dear.

(Wrestling to get free, she knocks his hat off.)

GLORIA

Let go of me.

ZEUS

I will transport you to heights of ecstasy you have never before experienced.

GLORIA

Not me you won't mister.

> (She knees him in the groin, takes his arm and gives him a judo flip over her hip. When he starts to get up, she delivers a chop to the back of his neck that sends him sprawling. MARBURY enters.)

Oh, Marbury…

> (She rushes to him, and he takes her into his arms.)

MARBURY

You're shaking.

> (She clings to him tightly.)

What happened?

GLORIA

This awful man, he…he attacked me.

MARBURY

What?

> (He starts to go for ZEUS, but GLORIA restrains him.)

GLORIA

Just hold me for a minute.

(*He embraces her. She turns her face up to him, the fright clearing from her eyes.*)

Thanks. I need someone strong to protect me.

MARBURY

You know I'm always ready when you need me.

GLORIA

Europeans may dress fancy but it's only to cover the beast underneath.

MARBURY

I'm glad you've finally found that out.

CANDOO

Here's your glass. You need a drink after all that.

GLORIA

You can keep it. I don't need booze anymore.

(*She looks up at MARBURY. Their heads slowly come together. The kiss that follows is a long and tender one. Arm in arm, they exit.*)

CANDOO

(*To ZEUS.*)

I should have told you not to tangle with her. The last guy who tried got his arm broken.

ZEUS

(Rising.)

That creature is a woman? She has the disposition of a goat, the kick of a mule, and the strength of an elephant. She is the only woman who has ever resisted my magic rose.

CANDOO

They don't go for that hearts and flowers stuff anymore.

ZEUS

I will have to take her by force. No woman can defy Zeus in his desires.

CANDOO

There are other ways. She's still a woman you know.

ZEUS

You are an expert in these matters?

CANDOO

I know an approach that's guaranteed to succeed.

ZEUS

Tell me, what is it?

CANDOO

Untie me, and I will.

ZEUS

Your arrogance has gone to the extreme of hubris. You have arrogated to yourself the power of the gods. This cannot be allowed.

CANDOO

Do you want this woman or don't you?

(ELENA enters.)

ELENA

Father, do not listen to this man. He is not to be trusted.

ZEUS

He claims to have magical ways with women.

ELENA

At a time like this, duty demands that you suppress your baser instincts and discharge the responsibility that is yours as the king of the gods.

ZEUS

Listen to a woman and she tells you you must behave like a eunuch. What is the point of being a god if you can't do whatever you want?

ELENA

There is a time for that, but now you must be strong and resolute.

ZEUS

I <u>must</u> nothing. I will do as I will.

CANDOO

You know, I've been thinkin'. If you and me joined together, we'd make one helluva combination. With my entrepreneurial genius and your magical powers, we could build Candooco into a mighty worldwide company in no time.

ZEUS

Candooco?

CANDOO

That's the name of my company. I'm the President. You can be Vice President in charge of personnel.

ZEUS

Personnel?

CANDOO

People. You get the employees charged up to work hard by offerin' them all kinds of goodies if they perform and rain all over 'em if they don't.

ZEUS

I know nothing about these things.

CANDOO

Won't make any difference. Just pump up the troops at sales meetings and zap 'em with fiery memos when they're layin' down on the job.

ZEUS

Memos?

CANDOO

Notes you send out on the Internet.

ZEUS

I...I don't know how to write.

CANDOO

No problem. You dictate what you want to say and a secretary will type it up for you.

ZEUS

Secretary?

CANDOO

A woman who answers your phone, handles your correspondence, arranges your appointments, gets your coffee. A good one will take care of everythin' you need,

ZEUS

Everything I need?

CANDOO

If you treat her right.

ELENA

Father, he is just trying to trick you into freeing him.

CANDOO

If you turn down this offer, you'll end up a miserable bum again. But if you come in with me we'll build Candooco into a giant multinational corporation, with thousands of employees, hundreds of thousands, and all of 'em dependent on you for their jobs. They'll respect you, fear you, kiss your ass, do anythin' you say. They'll worship you just like the Greeks did back in the good old days.

ZEUS

I speak and men listen? I command and they obey?

CANDOO

They better or you fire 'em.

ELENA

Do not listen to him. He only wants to use you to suppress his people for his own selfish purposes.

CANDOO

This company of ours will stretch across the entire world.

ZEUS

Beyond India?

CANDOO

You betcha. Bangkok, Singapore, Shanghai...

ZEUS

Alexander only got as far as India.

CANDOO

Alexander? Alexander is nothin' compared to what we can do.

ELENA

Father, you cannot lend your power to this awful barbarian.

ZEUS

With him, we can create a new Hellenic empire that will spread the spirit of Hellas to the farthest corners of the earth.

ELENA

He knows little and cares nothing about our values and virtues.

ZEUS

You can teach him. The ideas of Socrates, Plato, and Aristotle will transform him into a wise and noble leader.

(ZEUS exits. CANDOO'S cell phone rings.)

ELENA

What's that?

CANDOO

It's my phone, over there by the chair.

(ELENA picks it up.)

Tell 'em I'm all tied up. Push the little button at the top.

ELENA

It's a woman, your wife.

(She hands him the phone.)

CANDOO

Who answered the phone? It's...I don't know who she is. She just wandered in. She's young, yes. Pretty? She's Greek. Look, there's nothin goin' on, I'm too busy takin' care of the business. You what? Want a divorce? Billy Bob? You're in love with Billy Bob Boggess. But he's gay. You know? How do you know? That no good double crossin' son of a bitch. Yeah, yeah, I know. It's been too long. No, I'm tellin' you, I don't even know her name. You know I don't have any money. It's all tied up in the business. Your lawyer? We don't need lawyers to settle this. Oh come on Mabel...She hung up. My wife's in love with another man. Billy Bob Boggess, the biggest gold digger in Houston. And I thought he was gay.

ELENA

Gay?

CANDOO

Queer, a homosexual. A guy who likes men...more than women. She'll try to get everythin' out of me she can.

ELENA

But she's your wife. She can't, she can't just go off with another man, can she?

CANDOO

In our country, she can.

ELENA

We would never allow such a thing. A woman is bound to her husband for life.

CANDOO

Times have changed. Women are free to do about anythin' they want to these days.

ELENA

But don't you love her?

CANDOO

Love? Love is somethin' that seems to come and go. After a while, the grass seems to be greener on the other side of the fence.

ELENA

The fence? I do not understand.

CANDOO

It's just an expression we use. It means people get tired of what they have and want somethin' different.

ELENA

If had a man I loved, I would never let him go. I think I would, if love is as powerful as they say it is.

CANDOO

It is powerful, especially in the beginning. A man and a woman, they are attracted to each other, they want to get to know each other better. They hold hands.

(He takes her hand.)

They look into each other's eyes and see somethin' that draws them even closer together. He touches her hair, caresses her cheek. She smiles. He says something.

ELENA

What? What does he say?

CANDOO

It depends. He knows how he feels but he's not sure if she feels the same way.

ELENA

This is all so new to her.

CANDOO

Next comes this.

(He kisses her lightly. She backs off.)

She backs away, frightened and confused.

ELENA

She has never done this before.

CANDOO

Then she needs to experience one with true feeling.

(He embraces her and kisses her. She gasps for air but continues the kiss. They finally break apart.)

She is now maybe not so frightened.

ELENA

It is perhaps like learning to drink wine. The first sip is very strange.

CANDOO

But you soon get to like it.

ELENA

I don't know.

CANDOO

What is your name?

ELENA

Elena.

CANDOO

Elena.

ELENA

It means I am a daughter of Hellas, of Greece.

CANDOO

Elena.

(He kisses her again.)

ELENA

I feel a tingling sensation all over.

CANDOO

Good. You're learning.

ELENA

But like too much wine, it can be dangerous.

CANDOO

Yes, but it takes a lot of wine before you lose control.

ELENA

Not if you're not used to it.

(He kisses her again.)

Please, we must stop.

CANDOO

Why?

ELENA

You are a barbarian. I am a Greek.

CANDOO

But your father says you are to teach me how to be a Greek.

ELENA

<u>He</u> will have to do that.

CANDOO

And I can teach you about love.

ELENA

Love? No, only mortals can love. You have a wife. She may change her mind.

CANDOO

Mabel? No way. Once she makes up her mind, that's it.

ELENA

I know very little about you, and what I know I do not like.

CANDOO

Your father has ordered you to educate me in the ways of Greece, so here's your chance to change me into someone more to your likin'.

ELENA

I do not think it is possible.

CANDOO

My philosophy is that anything is possible if you want it bad enough.

ELENA

A typical barbarian way of thinking.

CANDOO

Well let's start and see who's right. First thing you do is untie me.

ELENA

I explained, I cannot set you free. Only my father can do that.

CANDOO

Come on, he has put me into your hands.

ELENA

You must promise to follow my instructions.

CANDOO

I promise.

(She unties the rope. He coils the rope and throws it aside.)

Okay now here's what we're gonna do. Go get your father. I want to put him to work right away.

ELENA

No, we must start your education in how to be a Greek.

CANDOO

Not now deary. I've got urgent business to do.

ELENA

But you promised.

CANDOO

A man has a right to do anything to get his freedom back, something you may not understand but I'm sure your father would.

ELENA

A man who breaks his word is worse than a thief. My father will punish you severely for this.

(She exits. ARTHUR enters.)

ARTHUR

Pop, I'm sorry. I didn't know Dr. Bend was a complete nut case.

CANDOO

You put him up to this. You and Marbury have been working behind my back to get rid of me so you can take over the company.

ARTHUR

No, it was my idea. Marbury had nothing to do with it. For him, you're still the boss.

CANDOO

If you'd been patient, I would have taught you the business and then you'd have been ready to take on more responsibility.

ARTHUR

But you said you were never going to…quit the business.

CANDOO

It's goin' to get bigger and I'll need a lot of help as it expands. But right now I'm sendin' you back home. Your mother has decided she wants a divorce.

ARTHUR

A divorce?

CANDOO

She's fallen in love with Billy Bob Boggess.

ARTHUR

Billy Bob Boggess, but he's gay.

CANDOO

That's what I thought, but she says it's not true. I guess he's just been pretending so he can fuck half the wives in Houston and get away with it. Here's what I want you to do. Go home and see that they don't ruin the company in the divorce proceedings. He's obviously after her for her money and will try to loot the company for all he can get.

ARTHUR

Billy Bob Boggess. I can't believe it.

CANDOO

Snoop around and dig up some dirt on him. I'm sure there's a lot. Hire a private eye if you have to. You do a good job and I'll bring you back into the company.

ARTHUR

I'll see what I can do.

CANDOO

I don't want you to see if you can, I want you to do it.

ARTHUR

Okay, it's a deal.

(He exits. ZEUS enters carrying his thunderbolt and his "King's" outfit without the hat.)

ZEUS

There are no women anywhere.

(ELENA enters.)

ELENA

I am here father.

ZEUS

Elena my dear, but you're not what I need right now.

ELENA

He is free now and returning to his old arrogant ways.

(ZEUS mounts the steps.)

You must command him to take instruction from me about our Greek virtues and values.

ZEUS

I so command.

CANDOO

Wait a minute. I'm still the boss here.

ZEUS

Am I not in charge of all the people?

CANDOO

I explained that. I'm the President and Chief Executive Officer of Candooco. You're only a department head. You report to me.

ZEUS

I am Olympian Zeus, king of the gods. I take orders from no one.

(ZEUS raises his thunderbolt. A violent storm ensues. The stage goes dark, punctuated by flashes of lightning and peels of thunder. A strong wind blows CANDOO to the ground. ZEUS enters the temple. ELENA crosses to CANDOO.)

ELENA

Are you all right? Let me help you up.

CANDOO

I'll just…lie here…a minute, storm…knocked the wind out of me.

ELENA

My father can be very violent when he is angered.

CANDOO

Yeah.

ELENA

He will become even more angry if you persist in your arrogant ways.

CANDOO

He wants to fight, let's do it fair and square, man to man.

(He tries to sit up. She helps him.)

Owww. It hurts. Right here *(taps his left chest)*.

ELENA

You have learned the first lesson in becoming a Greek. You can never be as powerful as the gods.

CANDOO

Take that thunderbolt of his away and we'll see.

ELENA

But as a mortal you can feel and experience things the gods can never enjoy.

CANDOO

(Gripping his chest.)

Owww. It's like a kick from a wild horse.

ELENA

You can savor every moment because time is so precious.

CANDOO

My father died at 50 of a heart attack. I've always said that couldn't happen to me.

ELENA

You don't know how lucky you are.

CANDOO

Maybe we should call a doctor.

ELENA

I'm sure my father won't allow it.

CANDOO

What do you mean? I may be having a heart attack.

ELENA

This is your punishment.

CANDOO

Bull shit.

(He stands, swoons and leans on ELENA for support.)

ELENA

You're learning. You've got to rely on other people. You can't do everything by yourself.

CANDOO

Cut the sermons and give me my cell phone.

ELENA

I don't know where it is.

CANDOO

It was right by the chair.

ELENA

It's not there.

CANDOO

Damn it.

(He sinks into the chair.)

ELENA

I'll go ask my father. Perhaps I can get him to relent.

(She exits. CANDOO tries to stand up but collapses back into the chair. GLORIA and MARBURY enter.)

GLORIA

Arty, we've got wonderful news. Marbury and I are going to get married.

MARBURY

Just as soon as we can get somebody to marry us.

CANDOO

(Sourly.)

Congratulations.

GLORIA

Is that all you can say?

CANDOO

What do you want me to say?

GLORIA

You could congratulate us and wish us all the best for a long and loving future.

CANDOO

Lots of luck.

GLORIA

We'll have to go back to Houston where we can have a really great party.

MARBURY

I called my ex-wife and she said she's delighted. She didn't think I'd ever find another woman who'd marry me.

GLORIA

And here I was, right here all the time.

MARBURY

I kept telling her she needed someone who saw the wonderful person she was underneath that vulgar facade she kept presenting to the world.

GLORIA

Vulgar?

MARBURY

You could be very crude when you were drinking.

GLORIA

Crude?

MARBURY

I mean it wasn't really you. But you're better now that you've stopped drinking.

GLORIA

Oh?

MARBURY

You're okay, you're fine, you're wonderful.

(He gives her a quick kiss.)

Let's not worry about the past.

GLORIA

Arty, you're white as a sheet. What's the matter?

CANDOO

I'm having a heart attack.

GLORIA

A heart attack?

CANDOO

That storm knocked me on my ass.

MARBURY

Yeah, it was something. We had a hard time getting up here.

CANDOO

I've got pains in my chest.

MARBURY

My father was a doctor. Let me feel your pulse. Seems to be normal.
(He feels CANDOO's brow.) No fever.

CANDOO

I can't find my phone to call a doctor.

GLORIA

I'll go get Security.

(She exits.)

MARBURY

Where does it hurt?

CANDOO

Right here.

MARBURY

That's awfully low down to be you heart.

CANDOO

Goddamnit I may be dying. Get me a doctor.

MARBURY

You said you weren't going to…

CANDOO

Marbury for Christ's sake.

MARBURY

Okay, okay.

(*MARBURY exits. ELENA enters.*)

ELENA

My father says he will let you see a doctor if that is what I wish.

CANDOO

So get goin'. I'm having a heart attack.

ELENA

If I do this, I need something from you.

CANDOO

I'll turn into a nice good-guy Greek just like you want me to.

ELENA

I want you to teach me more about love.

CANDOO

Love?

ELENA

You showed me how it starts, but then what happens?

CANDOO

Look, just get me a doctor. We can talk later.

ELENA

I cannot trust your promises.

CANDOO

I'll soon be dead.

ELENA

You are different now. You have changed. You no longer want to be a god. You have learned that you are not as powerful as you thought you were.

CANDOO

So go ahead and let me die.

ELENA

(Kneeling beside him.)

I don't want you to die.

(She leans over and kisses him.)

After you first kissed me, I have felt a smoldering fire inside I have never experienced before.

(She presses against him. He cries out in pain. She feels where it hurts, rubs her hand across it.)

You have a cracked rib.

CANDOO

How do you know? You're not a doctor.

ELENA

I have much experience with injuries. One of my duties has been to visit and console our wounded and dying soldiers.

CANDOO

What do we do about it?

ELENA

Nothing. You take it easy and get lots of rest and it will cure itself. I know it will be difficult but I will help you.

(She kisses him. He responds little to her ardor.)

We'll get you well very soon.

CANDOO

I still need to see a doctor.

ELENA

You do not believe me?

(He reaches over and kisses her. Surprised, she pulls back.)

CANDOO

Yes, I need you.

(She kisses him. They embrace warmly.)

Easy, you're goin' to break another rib.

ELENA

I'm sorry. What happens next, after a kiss?

CANDOO

I say you are a very lovely young woman.

ELENA

Only my father ever tells me that.

CANDOO

But you would be even lovelier if you weren't so serious all the time.

ELENA

There is so little pleasure in my life. I do not know how to be happy.

CANDOO

You can start with a smile.

(She tries to smile.)

Come on, you can do better than that.

ELENA

One has to have a reason to smile.

CANDOO

(Caressing her cheek.)

You're like all these old Greek statues, beautiful but with such hard stony faces. I wonder what would happen if you went up and tickled them?

(He moves his hand down and tickles her ribs. She breaks into a delightful laugh.)

It's like the sun coming out on a cloudy day. Just think about all the positive things you've got goin' for you. You're intelligent, curious, eager to learn, a talented woman who could do anythin' if she tried.

ELENA

No, you do not understand. In the world of the gods, I have to do whatever I'm told.

CANDOO

I say you can be whoever you want to be. Look how I perked up your father by getting him to believe in himself again.

ELENA

He wanted to regain his power as king of the gods. I want to experience all the joys that life can provide, but those can only be experienced if you are a mortal.

CANDOO

If you're a mortal, you die.

ELENA

If I could be free to love, and be loved, I would welcome death.

CANDOO

Is it that bad? No wonder you never smile.

(He tickles her again.)

ELENA

Please stop. I can't stand any more.

CANDOO

If that bothers you, you better think twice about becoming a human when you would experience a lot more thrilling sensations than that.

ELENA

I do not understand.

CANDOO

Don't the gods ever have sex?

ELENA

Have sex?

CANDOO

Get together for a romp in the hay? (Pause.) Copulate. Have babies.

ELENA

I've been told they did that back in the glory days, but that was a long time ago.

CANDOO

Boy, things really are bad.

ELENA

It's a never-ending torture.

CANDOO

You'll have a lot of adjustin' to do, a lot to learn.

ELENA

And you must teach me.

(ZEUS enters.)

ZEUS

The barbarian king is still here.

(ZEUS starts to raise his thunderbolt.)

ELENA

No father, he is no longer a barbarian.

ZEUS

Once a barbarian, always a barbarian.

ELENA

I am turning him into a Greek, but he is hurt and needs medical attention.

ZEUS

Provide him with whatever he needs but he must leave this sacred hill immediately.

ELENA

Father, there is something I must speak with you about.

ZEUS

Then speak.

ELENA

It is a private matter. I must see you alone.

ZEUS

You look so sad. Is something wrong?

ELENA

Come and I will tell you.

(They exit. GLORIA and MARBURY enter.)

GLORIA

You know what, these goddamned Greeks won't allow a doctor to come up here. They say, you bought the Acropolis, you should have your own doctor. I threatened them with everything I could. I said we'd tear down their fucking Parthenon if they wouldn't send us a doctor, but it didn't do any good.

MARBURY

They really do hate us.

CANDOO

It's okay. Turns out I only have a cracked rib.

GLORIA

How do you know that?

CANDOO

I can feel it.

GLORIA

Feel it?

CANDOO

Yeah, right here.

GLORIA

We'll fly in Dr. Klein. He's the best doctor in Houston. He'll make sure you're all right.

(CANDOO slowly rises.)

MARBURY

Can we help you?

CANDOO

I'm okay.

(He takes a step, grimaces with pain.)

I gotta go lie down and get some rest.

(MARBURY and GLORIA help him offstage left. ZEUS and ELENA enter.)

ELENA

Father you do not know how miserable I am. My life is nothing but endless days of drudgery and boredom.

ZEUS

You are the daughter of Zeus, an honor above all others and for which you should be proud.

ELENA

I am Father, but no one believes in you anymore.

ZEUS

They will, they will as soon as I show them that I am all powerful again.

ELENA

You have regained your strength. You do not need me anymore.

ZEUS

You have given me your undivided loyalty and support through all these terrible years and you must continue to do so in the future.

ELENA

I ask you, I plead with you to consider my situation. I cannot go on being a slave to the gods, subject to their every whim and cruel caprice. I want to have a life of my own. I would like to have a home, a husband, and children, all that the least of mortals enjoy.

ZEUS

You are my most prized possession Elena. Without you, I have no one who admires and respects me for what I am and not for the power that I wield.

ELENA

I have learned about a wonderful thing that mortals are capable of, something that makes them burn with a passion, a longing, a need that we know nothing of. It is called love.

ZEUS

Love?

ELENA

It forces you to think of someone outside yourself, to cherish them, to want to be with them, to share their jokes, to, to...

ZEUS

These things pass my dear daughter. They come like a spring shower and are gone just as quickly.

ELENA

But I must have them Father. I cannot go on without them. If you care for me, truly care for me, you will grant me this wish.

ZEUS

You would find that as a mortal you might experience happiness for a short period but then it comes to an end. Approaching death, you would plead with me to bring you back here, but I would be powerless to do so. You would lose your life and I would lose you. I cannot grant you this wish.

ELENA

If you loved me as mortals love, you would free me from this endless, meaningless existence and let me move into their world and enjoy all that they have, yes for what seems to us a short period, but to them is time enough.

(CANDOO enters.)

CANDOO

Can you all cut the chatter. I'm tryin' to get some rest.

ELENA

Tell him, tell him about love.

CANDOO

What?

ELENA

I have asked him to transform me into a mortal so I can experience love, but he doesn't understand.

CANDOO

Your daughter is very unhappy with her present life.

ELENA

That's what I've tried to explain to him.

CANDOO

She's heard about love and is just now beginnin' to know what it's like. You've got to feel it to know how powerful it can be, like a goat buttin' you head on.

ELENA

Father, hear what he is saying.

CANDOO

You've locked up your daughter here in a prison that's keepin' her from enjoying all the joys of life. With every day just like every other day, she's got nothin' to look forward to, nothin' to get excited about. Let her become a mortal and she can experience happiness and sorrow and most of all the wonders of love which you gods can never know. Yes, we mortals will die, but if dyin' is the price of the gift of love, we're more than willin' to pay it.

ZEUS

It's understandable that you've created this fantasy to enable you to be content with your short life, but I will not allow my daughter to give up eternal life for a few brief moments of happiness.

ELENA

But Father please, I do not want to go on living without any hope of ever being happy.

ZEUS

This is a matter for me to decide.

CANDOO

Look Mister Zeus, I made you and I can break you.

(ZEUS starts to raise his thunderbolt. CANDOO stops him.)

I'm the only person who believes in you. If I stop, you'll go back to bein' nothin' but a down and out drunken bum.

ELENA

He's right Father. You know what a miserable life you've had since the Golden Age.

ZEUS

But you believe in me. That will give me strength.

ELENA

No. I will, not help you anymore.

ZEUS

You must. You are my daughter.

CANDOO

You've sure got to be a very cruel and selfish father to deny your daughter this request.

ZEUS

I will decide what's best for her. This is no concern of yours.

CANDOO

But it is. She's taught me a great deal, changed my thinkin' about a whole lot of things. We humans are not gods, and it's crazy to think we are, not only crazy but dangerous. It makes us arrogant and power-mad, makes us want to do things to satisfy our own egos instead of doin' what's good for everyone. And she's taught me somethin' else. I was in love once, a long time ago. I thought I could live without it, but she's showed me that I was wrong. Sharin' your life with someone else is far more important than just bein' rich and powerful. She keeps talkin' moderation and all that Greek stuff about not carryin' anythin' to extremes, but what I see is a beautiful, intelligent woman who needs someone to show her my world that's full of joy and sorrow, happiness and despair, beauty and chaos, laughs and tears, a world full of surprises and never a dull moment. She believes somethin' very few people do nowadays. She believes in love, and that's what makes her very special. And she brings out the best in me which I didn't know was there. What I'm tryin' to say is that I love her, I'm goin' to marry her, make her my wife.

(He embraces a rather startled ELENA.)

133

ZEUS

You do this and you'll have to leave the Acropolis and never return.

ELENA

Don't worry Father. We'll always believe in you and spread the word that you are still the father of the gods.

CANDOO

I'll sell the Acropolis to the Greek government for what I paid for it. We'll go back to Texas, settle down and have a couple of kids. I'll teach them the oil business so they can grow up and help run the business the way it should be run.

(ELENA embraces him warmly.)

ELENA

And you'll teach me how to be a good American wife.

CANDOO

No, I want you to learn the oil business too.

(ZEUS raises his thunderbolt, stirring up a storm. Thunder and lightning. A strong wind strips the toga from ELENA, revealing an attractive modern dress underneath, and drives her into CANDOO's arms. The storm subsides. ZEUS disappears into the temple. GLORIA and MARBURY enter.)

GLORIA

That was quite a storm.

(CANDOO and ELENA continue their embrace.)

Arty, what the hell. Who is this woman?

CANDOO

This is my fiancee.

GLORIA

Your what?

CANDOO

The woman I'm going to marry.

GLORIA

You're already married.

CANDOO

Mabel is divorcing me to marry Billy Bob Boggess.

GLORIA

Billy Bob Boggess, that fag.

CANDOO

She says not so, and she should know.

GLORIA

Oh my god.

MARBURY

Where did this young lady come from?

CANDOO

From heaven.

MARBURY

From heaven?

CANDOO

She didn't like it up there so she's coming down here with us.

GLORIA

Come on Arty. Tell us the truth.

CANDOO

Her name is Elena. She's giving up a lot to be here, so be nice to her.

GLORIA

(To ELENA.)

He often has delusions of grandiosity like this. I hope you can bring him down to earth.

CANDOO

She's learned that you have to die in order to love, a lesson we all should never forget.

MARBURY

I don't understand.

GLORIA

Arty, what's come over you? You're not making any sense.

CANDOO

Listen to Elena and you'll learn a great deal.

MARBURY

I hope she's not as confused as you seem to be.

CANDOO

She's a very wise woman. She's Greek after all.

GLORIA

Does she speak English?

CANDOO

Yes, very well.

ELENA

I look forward to joining you in Texas and becoming a loving member of your family.

MARBURY

We're going back to Texas?

CANDOO

Yep. I'm selling the Acropolis back to the Greek government and we're all goin' home where we belong.

MARBURY

What about the oil?

CANDOO

It'll be there whenever the Greeks want it.

GLORIA

Then there's nothing to keep us here in this god-forsaken place.

CANDOO

Right.

MARBURY

(Taking GLORIA's hand.)

We can schedule a wedding maybe next week.

CANDOO

At my ranch. All four of us. A double wedding made in heaven.

(They exit to the music of Mendelssohn's Wedding March.)

END OF PLAY

CANDOO!

A Brief Afterword

Since the idea that death enables us to love is an unusual concept, perhaps some elaboration will help in understanding it.

Death is unavoidable, but the prospect of finite life is a blessing because it moves us to produce, to create, to strive, and, best of all, to love.

As Elena explains, if one is immortal, nothing is important, nothing has any meaning. As the sun crosses the sky, "I don't seem to care. Why today? Tomorrow is soon enough. And so it goes, year after year…you'll find that time becomes a torture. Day after day, dum, dum, dum, dum, dum, dum – it never speeds up or slows down. It is inexorable, implacable, a tyrant even the gods cannot escape."

She speaks from experience. "We immortals only know how to hurt each other. It's our principal way of passing the time. Pain is the only emotion we can truly feel."

The Greek gods have enormous power but use it to manipulate, overpower, seduce, and betray both mortals and their fellow gods, never to establish permanent bonds or anything that could be defined as love.

What is this emotion called love? An excellent definition is offered by James B. Nelson in his 1992 speech, "Relationships: Blessed and Blessing":

> *Love is rejoicing in the beloved's presence. It is the gratitude for the existence of the other. It is a reverence that does not try to swallow the other up or fashion the beloved into a replica of the self. Love is the profound satisfaction in everything that makes the other great and glorious.*

Love is a selfless passion for "the other," a fellow human being, regardless of that person's race, creed, color, religion, nationality, or sexual orientation.

The proposition presented here is that this life is the only one we'll have, that it is precious and sacred, to be enjoyed and treasured.

We create literature and art to enrich life and defy death. Eternal life would drain such efforts of meaning and make them unnecessary. Why bother? There's always tomorrow, but tomorrow never comes, just endless days devoid of purpose.

The gift of death spurs us to live to the fullest and to find the love we all need for complete fulfillment.